Against the pristine ahistoricism of certain book collectors—who idolize the cryogenic hygiene of unchipped jackets and unclipped flaps on books unmarked and better yet unread—Michael Hampton's study of 'inscription in the expanded field' revels in the afterlife of books as sites for further marking: abrasion, tear, crease, dismemberment, notation, vandalism, *et cetera*. Books here—whether witnesses or victims, martyrs or survivors—are recognized as special types of chronographs, in which handling marks time and records history.

Assembling a catalogue of (excerpted) catalogues, Hampton offers a distant reading that only ever focuses up close; the result is illuminating and poetic, summoning an atmosphere of bibliographic melancholy. But the story here is far from tragic, and *Against Decorum* chronicles the unpredictable miracle of the codex: like human bodies, books are simultaneously unbearably fragile and unimaginably durable.

Moreover, this bibliographic attention recognizes literature not as abstract 'works', or even undifferentiated editions, but rather as a constellation of singularities illuminated in unique, material copies. The implications for literary history and theory are broader still. If we often imagine reading as a disembodied and intellectual activity, here are the unforgettable reminders that every contact leaves a trace (even, as Matthew Kirschenbaum has argued, for digital literature)—and that every act of reading is a moment of contact. Handle carefully.

Craig Dworkin
Professor of English, University of Utah

Michael Hampton

Against Decorum

Contents

Adam Smyth

'Grubby handling': a foreword

In *Against Decorum*, Michael Hampton conveys a rich, centuries-long culture of book damage. *Against Decorum* is an exploration of the many ways in which the physical integrity of the printed codex is put under strain. A connoisseur of the frayed, the scuffed, and the torn, Hampton describes 'a new era of bibliographic unorthodoxy' in which books are fallen things.

Hampton's source for section 1, 'Register', is the contemporary bookseller's catalogue: a form of book description that in England grew out of the auctions that became popular in the last quarter of the seventeenth century. The first known public auction of books in England was held on 31 October 1676 when the library of clergyman Lazarus Seaman (d. 1675)—some 5,000 books—was sold at Seaman's former house in Warwick Lane, London. The auctioneer William Cooper seems to have modelled this sale and the 20 or so others he held before his death in 1689, on similar auctions in Leiden and Amsterdam across the seventeenth century. The catalogue that was printed to advertise the 1676 sale was an important document in the creation of a genre—alive today in the catalogues Hampton reads—characterised by a register of restrained celebration, and an attention to copy-specificity, completeness, uniqueness, rarity, and value. [α]

[α] R. C. Alston, *Inventory of Sale Catalogues of Named and Attributed Owners of Books Sold by Retail or Auction 1676–1800,* 2 Vols (Yeadon, Yorks.: Privately Printed for the Author, 2010). The Lazarus Seaman sale catalogue is *Catalogus variorum & insignium librorum instructissimae bibliothecae clarissimi doctissimiq viri Lazari Seaman, S.T.D. quorum auctio habebitur Londini in aedibus defuncti in area & viculo Warwicensi Octobris ultimo cura Gulielmi Cooper* (1676). The rise of a particular language of rarity, and its relation to early auctions, is explored most recently in David McKitterick, *The Invention of Rare Books: Private Interest and Public Memory, 1600–1840* (Cambridge: Cambridge University Press, 2018).

To these contemporary works Hampton brings a scalpel and excises a language of time-worn use. Hampton calls these excerpts 'gleanings', 'trawlings', and 'shards', among other things. The result is a piling up that is a kind of poem built from a language of book damage. From Catalogue 68 of Ken Spelman Rare Books in York (November 2010), what was a paragraph-long description of a copy of Joseph Moxon's *Practical Perspective, or perspective made easie, teaching the opticks* (1670), on sale for £280, is stripped back to 'Old [staining] to the text'. The description of a copy of William Austin's *A Specimen of Sketching Landscapes, in a Free and Masterly Manner* (1781), bound in half calf with a red morocco label and priced at £2,200, is redacted down to 'faint [waterstaining]'. And the description of an eighteenth-century handbill about Newmarket stage wagons, priced at £95, is clipped to '[show-through] of writing on the reverse'.

The discourse of book use buried in catalogues but raised to prominence by Hampton's cutting is teeming and strange. It is a language of chipping, foxing, staining, cracking, soiling, corroding; of the tipped-in, the oxidised, the creased, and the dusty; of the torn, the mottled, the thumbed, the cropped, and the nicked. Some of the terms ('embrowning') are beguilingly unusual. Some of them are erotic: there is a lot of 'rubbing', particularly at the 'extremities'. Sometimes books are like bodies (they might be 'sunned', as if on a beach in August); sometimes ('worming') books are a kind of food. There is a pathos in this, too, a sense that these signs of use mark the passage of time: the language of 'grubby handling' is (in Hampton's words) 'shot through with melancholy', and *Against Decorum* might be read as a poem about, and composed out of, bibliographical entropy. Bibliography—literally, 'book-writing'—is, in Hampton's hands, cut back to a vocabulary of the 'defective', the 'lacking', the 'fading', and the 'gone'.

But this world of damaged books is also rich with life: books are continually on the move, and the 'handling marks' they retain are a version of memory. With this sense of *books in motion*, Hampton's text catches three important attitudes towards the book within bibliographical studies of the last ten years or so. The first is that sense of books having *onward lives*. An older version of bibliography that dominated scholarship for much of the twentieth-century fixated on the moment of the book's original production, but this paradigm has been replaced, or revised, by a surge of interest in books *moving through time*; of books as social, even gregarious objects, passing between readers, circulating within communities, traveling to new lands, living on across generation after generation of owners, and down the centuries. Books, we realise, have long lives, and need not be locked in the punctual moment of publication.[β]

The second attitude is the idea of copy specificity: that notion that rather than discussing a book at the level of an edition (with the assumption that all copies within that edition-run are the same), we should think about each copy of a book as a distinct object, with its own quirks. We're long used to each manuscript being a unique thing, but the rise of copy-specific readings of print culture have encouraged us to think of each copy of a printed book as similarly distinct. This distinctiveness might be found in features of production, like stop-press corrections, or over-inking, or in binding; but it more often means attending to the layers of use acquired as books pass between readers: the marginal annotations, or the book-plates, or, more expansively, the bumps and stains and rubbings that Hampton gathers.

[β] Abigail Williams, *The Social Life of Books: Reading Together in the Eighteenth-century Home* (New Haven: Yale University Press, 2017).

Hampton here is in conversation with recent publications like Zachary Lesser's *Ghosts, Holes, Rips and Scrapes: Shakespeare in 1619, Bibliography in the Longue Durée*,[γ] which uses evidence such as ghost images, holes from stab-stitching, and page rips to tell new stories about the circulating, post-publication lives of books which we thought we already knew.

The third interest within recent bibliographical work that echoes in *Against Decorum* is the shift from histories of reading, to histories of book use. What do we do with books? We may read the text, but we often do other things too:[δ] we might use the margins for scribbling rows of financial accounts or shopping lists or (if we're a seventeenth-century Puritan) prayers; or we might display books to announce our learning or wealth or cultural capital or impeccable taste; or we might collect hundreds of books to furnish a room or (if we're an eighteenth-century aristocrat) to build a legacy; or we might use books as drinks coasters, or to keep a door ajar, or to hide behind in a public place.[ε] 'Use' is a more capacious term than 'reading' and can better respond to the book as an object as well as a text.

Hampton's 'gleanings' from book-dealer catalogues constitute the 'Register'. The second section of *Against Decorum*, 'Scrapbook', offers a series of quotations by novelists, poets, curators, book artists, antiquarians, scholars of book binding,

---

[γ]   Philadelphia: University of Pennsylvania Press, 2021.

[δ]   Leah Price, *How to Do Things with Books in Victorian Britain* (Princeton: Princeton University Press, 2012).

[ε]   On collecting to build a legacy, and on the need to think of book use beyond reading, see David Pearson, *Book Ownership in Stuart England* (Oxford: Oxford University Press, 2021). Pearson, seeking a focus on books as objects rather than texts, calls reading 'the r-word'.

historians of the book, and many others, that reflect variously on the physical book. Hampton's quotational method, shaped not only by Walter Benjamin but also by that earlier culture of Renaissance commonplacing, shows the long and lively history of book modification stretching across six centuries—accidental and purposeful; criminal and officially-sanctioned; public and private; joyful and embarrassed. The book modifiers in Hampton's world are as various as Elizabethan occultist John Dee, yBa Angus Fairhurst, seventeenth-century antiquarian Anthony Wood, 'frantic marginalist' Joseph Stalin, playwright Joe Orton and his partner-in-collage Kenneth Halliwell, businessman and book thief Farhad Hakimzadeh, French Renaissance essayist Michel de Montaigne, novelist Orhan Pamuk, bibliographer Katharine Pantzer, enthusiastic dog-earer Isaac Newton—and many more.

What we see is that books have never not been altered, and in place of the fantasy of the pristine volume, Hampton gives us an index—that is also a poem, and is also a manifesto—of handling, of wear and tear, of water-stained pages and insect damage. Books here are in the world, on the move, not behind glass, and in this culture, no person can definitively 'own' a book: the book always exceeds them, and the best we can do is feel it pass through our hands.

Michael Hampton

Author's note

Author's note

¶ The inter-related sections of *Against Decorum* comprise a 'superstructure' to use seventeenth-century librarian John Dury's term (i.e. a type of new knowledge), representing both the urge to edit in order to reconceive the given (in accord with information as material's motto of 'selecting and re-framing extant material to generate new meanings' [*sic*]), and also collect and mount quotational samples (didactic or otherwise) à la Walter Benjamin. Stripped down, the one word headings REGISTER and SCRAPBOOK are suggestive of the archivist's office and hobbyist's kitchen table, each function demonstrating my long standing fascination with the myriad ways imperfection, damage and entropy affect vintage books and especially library holdings (where disciplinary regimes often struggle to resist the forces of circulation, abuse, and decay, relying both on tacit decorum and rule-bound conventions), affecting their physical integrity and value. REGISTER in particular, is a modest contribution to the ever-growing terrain of post-Objectivist, conceptual writing, less minor *détournement* of the found, than a strategic removal, a wilful redaction of bibliographic hard data, disclosing hidden linguistic structures or Word-Reliefs. Reconceiving rare books from saleable items in a heavily coded dealer's list (ephemeral publications usually without ISSNs, which are periodic and often binned after use), to ontological indexes of handling, of wear & tear—ultimately analogues to the passage of time—unveils new contours for a meta readership no longer bound by user codes inherited from the Victorians, and piqued by the bibliographic curiosities to be found in SCRAPBOOK, which fall into the following basic groups: Accidental Loss, Marginalia, Weird & Wonderful, Wilful Damage. Altogether, the diverse samples presented in *Against Decorum* mark a new era of bibliographic unorthodoxy.

REGISTER A

it is no longer necessary to invent poetry,
instead it's a matter of locating it

Ulf Karl Olov Nilsson [*]

1.

Gleanings from Blackwell's summer catalogue **FIRSTS: one hundred recent acquisitions**, 2019. Blackwell's Rare Books, 48–51 Broad Street, OXFORD OX1 3BQ

Dustjacket [price-clipped]; [faded] backstrip panel; later ownership [inscription] to initial blank; [browning] to free endpapers; dustjacket with very minor [rubbing]; hint of [chipping] at head; [rubbing] to extremities; light [edge-spotting]; partial [browning] to free endpapers; minor [rubbing]; the odd tiny [nick]; ends of spine [bumped]; a few stray [pencil strokes]; small patch of [dustiness]; slight [wear] to extremities; [lean] to spine; top edge a trifle [dusty]; [spots] to endpapers; dustjacket a little [rubbed]; few faint [spots] to edges; [chipping] to extremities; faint [spots] to prelims; some minor [rubbing]; edges [untrimmed]; head & tail-pieces a bit [browned] and [spotted]; light handling [marks]; minimal [worming] in the lower margins of the first 4 gatherings; page with contemporary [annotations]; [tipped-in] note at end; a hint of [foxing][i] on the title page; spine slightly [faded]; upper cover slightly [rubbed]; endpapers [toned]; lower inner hinge [stained]; dustjacket [price-clipped]; edges [untrimmed]; minor [soiling] in places; tiny bits of [worming] in the lower margins; a little [cracking] to joints; headcaps [defective]; couple of minor [pen marks]; corners [bumped]; top-edge a trifle [dusty]; some headlines [cropped] though none eradicated; variously [browned]; [wax-stains]; spine slightly [cocked]; [toning] to backstrip panel; small pink [stain] at head of lower board; occasional [browning]; plates [spotted]; lightly [rubbed] at extremities; mild [damp-staining]; marginal [notes] in a miniscule hand; staples slightly [rusted]; spine ends [pushed]; small [tape stains] to boards; minor [water-staining]; faint [foxing] to free endpapers; a little [chipped]; the odd [nick]; trivial [wear] at head; minimal [underlining]; [erased] pencil lettering; faint blue ink [mark]; a bit [rubbed]; [bump] to one corner; short closed [tear] at head of backstrip panel; a little [frayed] around head; [speckled] edges; minor [chipping]; [drink-staining]; edges lightly [foxed]; very faint [offsetting] of the plates; a bit [discoloured]; label [damaged]; light [dust-soiling]; insect [damage] in middle of upper joint; [biro]; small bookseller ticket [W.H.Smith Paris] to rear pastedown; [nicked]; some [worming]; copiously [annotated]; faint [spots] to borders; trivial [knock] to top corners; [browned] around the edges; ownership [inscription] at head; a few [spots] to flyleaf; vestige of [string tie]; miniscule spot of [worming]; [cracks] to joints; [loss] of page numeral; headcap [defective]; small [split] at foot of spine; turn-ins a little [spotted]; very light [handling marks]; [price-clipped]; top edge [dusty]; a trifle [foxed]; a little [sunned]; internal [tape repair].

December 2019

2.

Bits & pieces from Paul Green's **Recent Imported and British Small Press Poetry together with A Number of Secondhand Acquisitions, A Catalogue for May, 1999,** 1999, and **Imported and British Small Press Poetry together with Recent Secondhand Acquisitions, An Interim Catalogue for November, 1998,** 1998. Paul Green, 83(b) London Road, PETERBOROUGH Cambs. PE2 9BS

Minor exterior [scuffing]; [price-clipped]; some [shelf-wear]; [tatty]; some [discolouration]; page edges [foxed]; top inch of the spine has a lightish [stain]; ex lib; [creased] cover corner; [scuffing]; [splits] to top and bottom of spine; gift [inscription]; slightly [wrinkled] dw; small [stain] somewhere; some [foxing] to prelims; text heavily [annotated] in pencil; no dw; both covers [chipped]; [wear]; [torn] and repaired dw; minor cover [rippling]; edges [browned]; [nicks] to dw; signs of [use]; slight front cover corner [fraying]; cloth in [tatty] but intact dw; top inch of the spine has a lightish [stain]; very small [mark] seems to be present on the front cover; [signed] by a previous owner; slight [fading] to spine and board edges; [clipped] dw; slight shelf [fading]; some edge [scuffing]; covers [browned] along edges; [lacking] dw; [discoloured] but intact; [fading] to edges of cover boards; pages [browning]; [chipping] to wraps; [tears] to dw; slightly [soiled] dw; heavily [annotated] in pencil; [faded]; small [wear]; [aged] but intact; somewhat [aged] dw; minor cover [rippling]; [browned]; [nicks] to dustwrapper; some effort made to [repair] the hinging; [fraying] to spine top of coverwrap; stapling [rusted]; [chipped] areas to book cover; top corner mail [bumped].

January 2020

3.

Fragments from James Fergusson's catalogue **Every Printed Page is a Swinging Door: books from the library of David and Judy Gascoyne**, 2011. James Fergusson Books & Manuscripts, 39 Melrose Gardens, LONDON W6 7RN

In memoriam Simon J. Miles 1956–2005

Some page [embrowning]; [scuffed] at spine; marginal [pencilling]; backstrip slightly [worn] at foot; [offsetting] onto free endpapers; slightly [faded]; rather [spotted]; dw [price-clipped]; mildly [faded]; some [rusting]; from staples; [inscribed] by the author on the half-title; upper joint a little [shaky]; early pages very [foxed]; several marginal [markings]; ownership [label] of David Gascoyne; dw [frayed]; one corner [creased]; spine slightly [nicked]; small ballpoint [squiggle] on final blank; light coffee [splashes] on upper cover panel; fore-edge roughly [trimmed]; spine slightly [creased]; covers rather [darkened]; dw [frayed] and defective in lower cover panel; covers slightly [spotted]; spine [darkened]; dw rather [worn]; [damp-marked]; autograph [corrections]; [tear] in lower panel; endpapers partially [embrowned]; mild [creasing]; tiny [spot] on upper cover; prelims a little [spotted]; [tape-repaired]; laminate on spine [lifting]; Tippex [erasures]; translator's autograph [deletion]; somewhat [faded]; ownership [label]; covers rather [thumbed]; [rough-trimmed] in binding; textual [underscoring]; rather [embrowned]; some [spotting] of prelims; backstrip slightly [torn] at foot; ballpoint [scribble] on last page; backstrip [defective]; spine [faded]; [rubbed]; glassine slightly [faded]; [bookplate] of Norfolk

County Library; staples a trifle [dusty]; spine slightly [rubbed]; free endpapers [embrowned]; coffee [stain]; covers mildly [mottled]; pages affected by [damp] at foot; small [dent] in the rear cover; backstrip [worn]; rear pastedown slightly [marked]; rather [soiled]; spine a bit [darkened]; traces of old tape [repairs]; hinges [cracked]; slightly [bumped] at one corner; [rubbed] at foot; slightly [foxed]; spine slightly [darkened]; free endpapers slightly [embrowned]; edge slightly [spotted]; glassine [torn]; fore edge [thumbed]; very [scuffed]corners; some [coffee-staining]; mild [crease] in backstrip; rather [foxed]; paperclip [rustmark]; [Tippexing]; ink [corrections]; [underscorings]; corners of final blank [creased]; spine [rubbed]; pencil [deletion]; backstrip [missing]; [faded]; slightly [darkened] at spine; covers [dirty]; [drawing] of elephant; some [foxing]; front panel [defective]; a short [tear]; mildly affected by [damp]; blue [marker] pen; staples [rusty].

February 2020

4.

Off-cuts from Benjamin Spademan's **Literature 1500–2000**, 2003.
Benjamin Spademan, 5a Brackenbury Gardens, LONDON W6 OBP

Sepia [annotations]; [faded] by 18th century washing;
small [hole] in lower margin of 3D4; text [soiled] with some
marginal tears; [repairs] to paper; slight [restoration] to head
and tail of spine; [wear] to extremities; slight [foxing] to
prelims; occasional light [browning and spotting]; [lacking]
half-title; some [wear] to joints; slight [stain] from pressed
flowers; [dampstain]; small piece [torn] from lower corners
of pages 249 and 271; minor [soiling]; small marginal [stains];
new running title supplied in the author's [hand]; spine
[darkened]; hinges [split]; two short clean [tears]; unobtrusive
[dampstain]; some [foxing] throughout; slight wear to head
and foot; contents [browned] as usual; minute [hole] in last
leaf; spine very slightly [darkened]; minor [repairs]; lightly
[browned] throughout; hinges [starting]; small [nick] to top
edge.

March 2020

5.

Amuses-gueules from Ben Kinmont's **Catalogue 15: Gastronomy— A Catalogue of Books & Manuscripts on Cookery, Wine, Rural and Domestic Economy, Health, Gardening, Perfume, & the History of Taste 1505–1879**, Fall 2016. Ben Kinmont, Bookseller, 684 North Main Street, SEBASTOPOL, CA 95472

[Disbound]; [shadowing] from illustrations; one [wormhole] to the upperboard; slightly [sunned]; half inch [tear] to right edge of upper wrapper; endpapers [browned]; [soiling] to final two leaves; marginal paper [repair]; light [foxing]; [faded]; faint ex-library [stamps]; [sunned]; tiny rust [hole] to one leaf affecting two letters; evidence of [erased] pencil on the recto of upper wrapper; cancel slip [pasted] on imprint information; "good" [handwritten] in blue ink; light [foxing]; lavender illustrated dust jacket with some [wear]; [chipped] at head of spine; minor [water damage] throughout; pages [yellowed]; price [clipped]; occasional light [foxing]; loose [signatures] in wrappers; slight [smudges] on slipcase; slight [rubbing] to the lower portions; spine [sunned]; light [spotting] due to use; [untrimmed] throughout; corners [bumped]; [dog-eared]; food [spotting] on several leaves; [disbound]; small marginal [tear] on p.311; [scribbling]; some [wear] to joints; minor [foxing] to wrappers; [damp staining] to first leaf along spine.

April 2020

6.

Tidbits from Nial and Margaret Devitt's **Catalogue 32: Children's Books**, 1995. Nial Devitt Books,[ii] Merrion House, 217 Leam Terrace, LEAMINGTON SPA, Warwickshire CV31 1DW

[Repaired]; spine bit [faded]; covers [rubbed]; minor [soiling]; one or two gatherings a little [pulled]; occasional [thumbing]; spine gilt very [dull]; unsightly price [erasure]; [waterstained]; some [spotting]; [frayed]; some [offsetting] from plates; hinges little [strained]; many pages are thick with the owner's [pencilled] translations; gutter of title [strengthened]; minor [wear]; corners [rubbed]; little [dusty]; spine extremities [worn] and shabby; some [spotting]; marginal [waterstaining] of prelims; [fingering]; tiny [nick] at top of spine; [no] slipcase; thumbnail [scuff]; spine gilt [oxidised]; a little [dull]; spine [relaid]; inner hinges strengthened with archive [tape]; spine [perished]; small Sellotape [marks] on free endpapers; [soiled] at fore-edge; some [spotting]; rough [erasure] on lower cover; [tear] in index leaf repaired; [worn]; one illustration crudely [coloured]; 5 leaves are certainly [missing]; staples [corroding]; spine [rubbed]; [recased]; [lacks] front endpaper; bookplate margins [defective]; [frayed]; vellum [discoloured]; endpapers [spotted]; some minor [fingering]; spine [worn]; slight [cockling] of cloth on upper covers; secured with silk ribbon now partly [perished]; ends of spine panel [chipped]; [creasing] to covers; spine rather [dull]; corners [worn]; a little [dusty]; inner hinges [cracked]; old [signature] on half-title; minor [mark]; spine gilt [dull]; lower cover slightly [cockled]; upper joint [broken]; one corner trifle [bumped]; some leaves [dogeared]; a little [chipped] at edges; [recased];

old [inscriptions] on top margin of title; spine [relaid]; price roughly [erased]; [foxing]; minor [spotting] of prelims; plates [foxed]; [thumbing]; smallish brown [stain]; slightly [speckled]; upper joint [broken]; edges [rubbed]; [frayed] dustwrapper; few minor [tears] closed; little [spotted]; has a [stain] tea?; name [erased] on front blank; minor [crease]; occasional light [soiling]; edges little [darkened]; joints [cracked]; minor [wear].

May 2020

7.

Granules from eBay seller **meldrew-man3**, a.k.a. Martin Meldrew,[iii] Cottage, REDHILL, Surrey RH1 4NB

Minor [wear]; rub [marks]; spine [chipped]; [crimping]; slightly [cocked]; tide [marks] to edges of the lining; joints are [rubbed]; spine with [fraying] and [splitting]; shelf [wear]; [darkening]; cup [mark]; [discolouration] to lower cover; numerous pages [pulling] or [straining] at the gutter; intermittent faint [toning]; brown [blemishes]; faint [foxing]; marginal [nick] or [ding]; joints are [rubbed]; mold [marks]; grubby handling [marks]; remnants of pencil [marks]; [pulling] at the gutter; tattered shelf [wear]; [baggy]; ink [staining]; minor [foxing]; heavy [spotting]; [scuff] to top front joint; [blemishes] to margins; backstrip is [lifting] at head; [scuffs] to corners; sticker [remnants]; rear end paper is [browned]; spine is a tad [faded]; small [hole]; minor [foxing]; faint [yellowing] to the margins; edges are roughly [trimmed]; slightly [bent]; [disbound]; fire [damage] to the title page; liquid [staining] to the lower inner margin; corners are [dog eared]; probably [ex-library]; coding in [pencil]; dye [run] to the end papers; 8vo is [gaping] at the gutter; [toning]; slight [loss] of text; [worming] to the edges; spine [darkened] and [perished]; sporadic small food [marks]; [gaping]; numerous [errors] in paging.

June 2020

8.

Leftovers from ANTIQUA's **Catalogue 23: POSTWAR ART—Modern Movements from 1945 to the 70s (Modern konst från 1945 till 70-talet)**, spring 2018. ANTIQUA Kommendörsgarten 22, S-114 48 STOCKHOLM, Sweden

[Damp] streak; light [wear] in nethermost margin; light [foxing]; slightly [browned]; tiny corner [scuffing]; red [stains]; trace of [removed] label; lightly [stained]; small ink [stains]; very lightly [scuffed]; unobtrusive [rubbing]; some [offset]; age [wear]; interior edge dust jacket with some [repairs]; small [chipppings]; weak ballpoint pen [scrawl]; some [browning]; external traces of [handling]; [loss]; [wrinkling] of front wrapper; [sunned]; light [stains]; weak corner [scuffing]; jacket slightly [edgeworn]; ineluctable [darkening] along the fold; [tanned]; tiny weak [stain]; minor [imperfections]; closed [tear] at back; small [repair]; thin [knife-cut] through rear wrapper closed with tape on inside; a few leaves at the end [loosened] from the staples; mild age [toning]; thumbtack [holes]; list of members [underlined]; a few tiny [rifts] in margins; minor [wear]; rubber rings have been [lost]; small [rupture].

July 2020

9.

Trawlings from Ken Spelman **Catalogue 68**, November 2010.
Ken Spelman Rare Books, 70 Micklegate, YORK Y01 6LF

Old [staining] to the text; light [foxing]; light marginal [browning]; [traces] of mounting; a little [clipped]; [dusty]; faint [waterstaining]; contemporary [corrections]; slight [foxing]; marginal [waterstain]; few leaves [browned]; scattered [foxing]; corners [worn]; [lacks] the final plate; contents [loose]; dust [marks]; corners [bumped]; a little [rubbed]; first and last leaves [dusty]; inner joints [worn]; edges [browned]; a little [dusty]; some [foxing]; rear board unevenly [faded]; spine [faded]; [rubbing] to the extremities; old [damp]; contents [loose]; spine a little [sunned]; some [foxing]; upper board [sunned]; a little [damp stained]; light [folds]; [foxed]; small [tear]; [bubbled] in places; old fold [marks]; corner is [clipped] on the final advert leaf; spine [rubbed]; [show-through] of writing on the reverse; some [browning]; outer sections [dusty]; edges [rubbed]; [deletions]; light [browning]; old [waterstaining]; [dusty]; head and tail of the spine [worn]; light [foxing]; one leaf [browned]; slight [foxing]; some [creasing]; [ink] calculation in the rear panel; endpaper [clipped]; [lacks] the front end paper; age [browning] to paper; corners [bumped]; some insect [damage]; name [torn] from on end paper; minor [kocks] to the board edges; some [worming]; one joint [cracked]; slight [slits] to the central fold; heads [chipped]; [disbound]; spine [faded]; some [pencillings] to the inner boards; pin [holes] to the blank corners;

August 2020

10.

Excerpts from Bernard Quaritch's **Catalogue 957**, 1976.
Bernard Quaritch Ltd, 5–8 Lower John Street, Golden Square,
LONDON W1R 4AU

Marginal [rules] in red added; one or two trivial [stains];
light brown [stain]; one headline [defective]; cutter's [mark];
[marginalia] in a minute hand; [gauffered]; fleur-de-lys
originally silver now [oxidised]; a few [wormholes]; some
leaves insignificantly stained and [scribbled] on; joints
[repaired]; [underlinings]; [rebacked]; minor [worming]; clean
[tears]; few margins [shaved]; minor [worming]; a few light
[stains]; several marginal [repairs]; front hinge [repaired];
inoffensive [spotting]; upper joint [cracked]; little [browned]
in places; minor [flaws]; one leaf just [shaved] at head;
[wormholes]; [dust-marked]; trivial [defects]; occasional
light [browning]; a little [foxing]; [waterstaining] at end;
[wormhole]; title very lightly [shaved]; a little light [browning];
slightly [worn] in folds; [thumb-marks] in lower corners
throughout; [lacking] the blank A1; [loss] of two or three
letters; [tear] in upper margin of one leaf.

September 2020

11.

Snippets from Thomas J. Symonds's **Catalogue of Rare Books, Manuscripts, Autographs & Works of Art**, n.d. Thomas J. Symonds Rare Books, PO Box 50765, LONDON NW6 9AU

Some [browning] and staining; marginalia in text; a few [wormholes]; a small patch of board [exposed]; [rubrication] throughout; [worming] towards beginning and end; hinges [cracking]; some [worming]; bottom half of spine [split] along crease; light [soiling]; a few [wormholes] to blank margins; paper [flaw]; slightly [creased]; title-page [soiled]; occasional [browning]; first few leaves a bit [ragged]; [thumbed] at outer corner; [tear]; early [marginalia]; [underlining] in two hands; pink spine [worn]; small [tear] at bottom of first leaf; [damp-staining]; marginal [worming]; slight [spotting] to title-page; light [browning]; slightly [dusty]; bottom joint [cracked]; somewhat [rubbed]; [offsetting]; light [age-yellowing]; some [foxing]; [worming] to inner margin; occasional light [spotting]; [loss] at head of spine; title-page slightly [dusty]; [spotting]; light [browning]; [waterstaining]; [misprint] 'Boxburgh'; slightly [soiled]; [stain] towards tail; [ragged] at edges; [soiling]; [darkening]; light [spotting]; [age-yellowing]; slightly [rubbed]; joints [cracked]; [wanting] centrepiece and cornerpiece bosses; [age-browning]; minor text [loss]; light [browning]; some [chipping]; [bumped]; [worn]; early paper wrappers [torn]; medium [browning]; [spotted]; [ragged] at margins; [soiling]; [spotting]; [paste-ins] found extensively throughout.

October 2020

12.

Shards from Arena Book's **Catalogue 12—Books on the Performing Arts**, 1982. Arena Books, SHELSLEY BEAUCHAMP, Worcestershire WR6 6RH

Sl [fxg] prelims; cvrs [gone]; frontis [loose]; [trn] dw; fep [mkd]; ep's [fxd]; wrpprs [browned]; pict bds [worn]; [rbbd]; sp [worn]; [ex lib]; w sm [nck] tp sp; sl [fxg]; fep [mkd]; v sl [fxing]; ends sp v sl [fdd]; ep's [fxd]; cvrs sl [rbbd]; [crse] tp cvr; wrpprs [brwnd]; cvrs little [rbbd]; cvrs sl [brwn] at edges; intermit [fxg]; sp [dknd]; sl [crse]; tp sl [sngged]; cvrs [fdd]; sm [splt] tp sp; edges rgh [cut]; sl [fxg]; [mk] p.107; edges [wrn]; cvrs [fdd]; hngs [plld]; cvrs [rbbd]; sm [mk] fr bd; occ [fxg]; cvr & end pp [wrmd]; in [trn] dw; sp [fdd]; [rbbd]; cvr sl [mkd]; sp sl [dknd]; [fxg]; prelims sl [fxd]; cvrs [dknd]; [fxg] ends & edges; sp [fdd]; wrpprs sl [rbbd]; fep badly [mkd]; sl [fxd]; intermit [fxg]; sm [crse] top fr bd; [fdd]; wrpprs [tatty]; sl [fxg]; [shkn]; [trn]; ends [rbbd]; wrpprs [brwnd]; fep [mkd]; [fdd]; cvrs v sl [mkd]; few pp badly [opened]; crnrs sl [crsd]; sp sl [dknd]; [rbbd] dw.

November 2020

* The epigraph on p.19 is taken from Nilsson's essay 'The Poetics of Trauma' in *Granta* #149, *Europe: Strangers in the Land*, specifically the passage that examines Charles Reznikoff's *Testimony*, the unfinished poem he worked on for over forty years, and the late masterpiece *Holocaust* (1975). In both these works Reznikoff employed a very hard edit on found material: law reports in the former, Nazi trial reports in the latter. *Against Decorum* uses a similar paring knife, and although the material is scarcely of the same order, it too is shot through with melancholy.

REGISTER B

THE JARNDYCE SPECIAL[†]

Current book-sellers' catalogues present a grave problem. Space forbids that they should all be retained, yet it is a sad wrench to part with them. No ephemeral literature approaches them in fascination.

A. N. L. Munby, **'Floreat Bibliomania'**

Deposits from **Catalogue Two Hundred**, Autumn 2012.
Jarndyce Antiquarian Booksellers, 46, Great Russell Street,
LONDON WC1B 3PA

For reading aloud by two performers:

Sl. [rubbing]; spine [faded] to brown; [browned]; clasp
[missing]; title page [dusted]; one old [fold]; sl. [dulled];
some sl. [creasing]; [dulled]; prelims v. sl. [spotted];
occasional [foxing]; sl. [cocked]; sm. [pinmark] at upper
margin; inoffensive damp [marking]; the odd [spot]; spine
a little [darkened]; heavily [foxed]; sl. [sunned]; corners
[bumped]; [perforated] library stamp of Hammersmith
Public Libraries; sl. nick; [creased] at head; rust [stained]
at end; marginal [tears]; plates [browned]; old water [mark];
[rubbed]; some sl. [dusting]; [foxing] to prelims; internal
[worming]; one old [fold]; marginal [tear] to leading blank;
first gathering sl. [loose]; sm. [hole]; roughly [rebacked];
in brown sheep; hinges [cracked]; [chipped] black wax seal;
old [folds]; tape [ties]; pencil [marking]; [defective]; minor
[dusting]; sl. [spotting]; sl. [rubbing]; [tear] without loss; the
odd [spot]; [dulled]; occasional sl. [foxing]; uneven [fading];
slightly [cocked]; sm. [nick] to spine; [creased; [tears] to
fore-edges; [chipped] at edges; [rubbed] at foot of spine.

---

† *The Jarndyce Special* Word-Relief on p.40 was composed as a unique exemplum, identical in method and form to the cycle of twelve pieces that make up the first part of Register, but chronologically distinct from them.

Its parts were chosen from **Jarndyce Catalogue 200**, which is hailed by Brian Lake in a bespoke Afterword as a landmark publication in the history of this noted bookseller, at its premises directly opposite the British Museum, London.

Since 1970 Jarndyce has specialised in 18th- and 19th-century literature, with Charles Dickens predominant naturally, but its lists have covered subjects as diverse as Yellowbacks, Women Writers and the novels of George Gissing. Lake also traces the design history of Jarndyce catalogues, from early lists knocked up on duplicators, via the IBM golf-ball to today's Apple Mac.

Number 67, entitled 'The Museum', posed as a bibliographic cabinet of curiosities, taking their catalogue itself into the realm of the artists' book, for here it should be remembered that Lynda Morris & Germano Celant's publication *Book as Artwork 1960/1972* (1972), aside from being a theoretical benchmark of the genre, was itself configured as a select <u>list</u> of the artists' books exhibited at Nigel Greenwood Gallery B.

As a key part of *Against Decorum*'s superstructure, *The Jarndyce Special* proves the conceptual methodology of Register can be applied to any antiquarian book dealer's list, as it uncovers what is in effect a buried index of passing time, and one unchained from topic; the condition of old books providing a rich source of entropic data as matériel.

SCRAPBOOK

'Do not cut your bodies for the dead, and do not
mark your skin with tattoos. I am the LORD.'

Leviticus 19: 28, **New Living Translation** (2015)

'A wide variety of objects are on display in the exhibition—
from graffiti on a Babylonian brick to a banknote with hidden
rude words'.

British Museum briefing notes for 'iObject'. See **New Art Examiner**,
Vol.33, No.3, January 2018

'A library is a rule-bound institution, but surely that regulation is there for us to push against too?'

www.nicoladale.com/uploads/1/0/3/6/10361696/2017_in_
conversation_with_michael_hampton_-_original.pdf

'*Scribble* indicates the track and form of a frantic writing, as well as the production of marks void of intended meaning, a kind of doodling or "squandering" to borrow a term from Roland Barthes.'

Peter Suchin, 'Notes on Notes', **Index, Scribble, Snapshot, Tract** (London: Kaleid Editions, 2009), p.4

'each title bears witness
to Harry's appalling librarianship:
The Story of Purfling; *Living with Alzheimer's*;
[…] back issues of *Button Collector*;
Dogfighter Monthly […]; *Mad Triste*;
*The Use of Leucotomy in the Treatment of
Pre-Menstrual Stress*; *16 RPM—a Selective Discography*;
Diabetic Desserts All the Family Will Love; *Origamian Specials*;
[…] *Urine—The Water of Life*; *The King's Gambit—Play it To Win*;
The Al Bowlly Songbook; *Beyond Dance—New Adventures
In Labanotation*; *The Volapük*[iv] *Scout Manual*; piles of old
sick-notes, unmarked exam papers, staff memoranda
on Portion Control, and risible stabs at the Unified Field Theory,
furtively mimeoed in the janitor's office in playtime; […] *I am
John's Prostate*; […] *You and Your Autoharp*; […] *Steal this Book*
(signed, some foxing of endpapers); Stanyhurst's *Virgil*;[v] […] Pye's
Analecta (uncut); […] the Bible they quietly pulped when the
proof-reader's shopping list turned up in Numbers; […] a grimoire
in horrible waxpaper; […] *Leechdom and Wortcunning*; […] and
Tatwine's[vi] gigantic *Aenigmae Perarduae*, the whole thing a triple
acrostic; […] a monograph on the storage of turnips; […] a pile of
misprinted erratum slips; […] the full print-run of *Gems of the Muse*,
Vol.9 (Buckfast Books); […] *What is Emotion?* by […]'.

Don Paterson, 'The Alexandrian Library', **Nil Nil** (London: Faber, 1993),
pp.29–32

'Some surviving copies include witnesses to their reader's presence in the form of pins, buttons, drink stains and candle wax, demonstrating, as Mayer writes, that "The physical *and* intellectual dimensions of reading anchored Shakespeare existentially"'.

Stanley Wells, 'Pushed by many hands: Drawing attention to those who experienced Shakespeare on the page', **Times Literary Supplement**, 8 March 2019

'Nearly all the books are chained. The chains are formed of rod-iron bent into a figure of 8, with one end twisted round the middle for strength. We know the date when the library was founded, and therefore of these rude chains—it was 1686. Each chain is about 3 feet long, and has at one end a ring like a curtain ring, which running along an iron rod, allows considerable play. Thus you can take any work from its place to a desk at a little distance and there consult it, but you cannot take it away. There must have been some advantage in this plan, or it would not have been generally adopted; but apparently great disadvantage must have been experienced also. If the chains were a check upon stealing the books, they were certainly no preventive against damage and mutilation, as many of the volumes unfortunately prove. To lug out a heavy volume by the cover doesn't tend to preserve the binding.'

William Blades on Wimborne Minster Library, in **Books in Chains and other Bibliographical Papers** (London: Elliot Stock, 1892), pp.9–10

'Many other zines are mimeographed and homemade, have either holes, burns, perfume, stapling, hand drawn illustrations, famous writers, cut ups and obscene or subversive contents but few if any have all of these elements. My Own Mag's complete assault on printed culture arguably makes it the prototype for the D.I.Y. and mimeograph publishing "revolution" of the ensuing decades.'

Jeff Nuttall, *My Own Mag* Nos. 1–17, Catalogue 1455, **Counterculture** (London: Maggs Bros Ltd, 2011)

'What's the experiment? asked Rosa. What experiment? asked Amalfitano. With the hanging book, said Rosa. It isn't an experiment in the literal sense of the word, said Amalfitano. Why is it there? Asked Rosa. It occurred to me all of a sudden, said Amalfitano, it's a Duchamp idea, leaving a geometry book hanging exposed to the elements'. [vii]

Roberto Bolaño, Natasha Wimmer (trans.), **2666** (London: Picador, 2009), p.195

'In the 70s the Arts Council & other funding bodies emphasised that their financial support was dependent on books that would fit the size of the bookshop shelf. When they used excuses not to fund the avant-garde, one found oneself exploring the nature of the book, knowing that the chance of it being sold via a shop was limited. The book became more of an object itself outside the market place, when sold it was probably at readings or bookfairs. A book like *Violations*, researching different aspects of that notion, found the finished object with its title page ripped in two, and the book sealed with two pieces of tape (one marked m, the other f) that needed to be broken to gain entry.'

Paul Buck, **a public intimacy (a life through scrapbooks)** (London: Book Works, 2011), p.47

'Books are an interdisciplinary medium.'

Karen Wirth, 'Re-Reading the Boundless Book', Charles Alexander
(ed.), **Talking the Boundless Book: Art, Language, and the Book
Arts** (Minneapolis, MN: Minnesota Center for Book Arts, 1995),
137–144 (p.144)

'Blake Bronson-Bartlett has been teaching Ronald Johnson's ARK in a book history course at the University of Iowa. HYPERLINK "https://twitter.com/floodeditions" I had students turn in marginalia, which they marked with post-it notes of different colors…'

Flood Editions, 3 May 2019. **@floodeditions**

'a group of gentlemen surrounding the famed gothic writer and eccentric Horace Walpole undertook the extra-illustration of volumes dedicated to biography, travel, and history'.

Megan Walsh. **www.sharpweb.org/sharpnews/2019/12/29/lucy-peltz-facing-the-text-extra-illustration-print-culture-and-society-in-britain-1769-1840/?pdf=1400** 'le spectateur est invitÉ À lire le livre, À continuer de BRÛLER les pages en enflammant les allumettes collÉes, À ajouter d'autres allumettes, À rÉduire le tout en cendres. IngrÉdients: allumettes ordinaires, allumettes dÉtonantes.' [viii]

Instructions to users of Bernard Aubertin's **Livre Brüler Et à Brüler** (1962–71) 'a library in Paterson, New Jersey, lost 20 pieces of antique furniture and bronzes and waited six years to report the loss to police. An Indiana library couldn't find four paintings by the German artist Julius Moessel and never even tried to collect the insurance. An audit in Long Beach, California, found that about an eighth of the city-owned art collection could not be accounted for. The New York Public Library is missing a handful of maps dating back to the 15th and 16th centuries—and didn't even notice it had lost one of Ben Franklin's workbooks, until the person who inherited it offered to sell it back to the library. (The NYPL is currently suing for possession.) The Chicago Public Library has lost the vast majority of the 8,000 books, some of them now rare and valuable, that were donated to the city in 1871 and made up the library's original collection. In 2011, the San Francisco Civic Art Collection wasn't even sure how many pieces were in its collection. How did this problem first come to light? Well, some of its valuable pieces were found basically just lying around in a dank, watery hospital basement'.

www.atlasobscura.com/articles/libraries-and-cities-are-terrible-at-keeping-track-of-art

'With the introduction of mechanical typesetting the simple misprint was joined by a more complex jumble known as Printer's Pie.'

Fritz Spiegl,[ix] Foreword to **What the papers didn't mean to say—a scandalous collection of clangers, misprints and other typographical disasters** (Liverpool: The Scouse Press, 1965)

'POD books represent a genuine hybrid of digital and analog processes: under the guise of the "traditional" book form, there is a complex ecosystem made of file formats, metadata, retail platforms, multiple connections to online stores and, sometimes, even YouTube book trailers, authors' blogs, etc. Sent through the regular postal system, the physical book is the tip of the iceberg of an infrastructure that takes advantage of digital printing, desktop publishing, PDF format, and Web 2.0. Therefore, POD is not a new technology in itself, but a fruitful combination of existing ones'.

Silvio Lorusso, 'Print-on-Demand—The Radical Potential of Networked Standardisation', in Danny Aldred & Emmanuelle Waeckerlé (eds), **Code—X: Paper, Ink, Pixel and Screen** (Farnham: bookRoom press, 2015), 03:47-03:58 (03:48)

Bacon, George Mackenzie.:
On the Writing of the Insane, with illustrations..
London: J. Churchill & Sons, 1870..
24 pages, IV plates; (8°)
Item is destroyed ˣ

Explore the British Library

'Gertrude Stein's basic way of writing was to perform her poetics in her texts. This performance is nailing her points and acting on an excerpt from *Poetry and Grammar*.'

Kamilla Jørgensen. **www.kamillajoergensen.dk/i-am-a-grammarian**

'Diaries, journals, jottings. Moleskine notebooks written in green ink. Marginalia in a copy of *Catcher in the Rye*. Joseph Stalin, you know, was a frantic marginalist. His annotated Nechaev is historically revealing and shamefully ignored by scholars.'

Nick Harkaway, **Gnomon** (London: William Heinemann Ltd, 2017), pp.44–45

'Alterations to the books themselves began with typed additions to internal plates pasted over the existing print; words were highlighted or altered, critical comment made, sometimes comical and occasionally mildly obscene. Biographies received replacement portraits, authors substituted for someone or even "something" else. Over time, more abstract treatment of whole covers developed with carefully matched paper types and continued through the interior of the books, collaging directly onto art plates themselves. Finally, newly written synopses started to replace publishers' originals.'

Ilsa Colsell, **Malicious Damage: The Defaced Library Books of Kenneth Halliwell and Joe Orton** (London: Donlon Books, 2013), p.27

'greasy handmarks, sunbleached spines, cracked bindings, books which fall open at a particular place, stains, dirt as life and life as dirt'.

seekers of lice, 'Invent the Present: Footnotes' in Richard Sawdon Smith & Emmanuelle Waeckerlé (eds), **The Book is A——Live!** (Farnham: bookRoom, 2013), 54–63 (p.59)

'The use of pins to fasten clothes is well known but it is clear that people used the pin in a variety of ways including in books. Their use as bookmarks or page markers has been noted.'

Caroline Duroselle-Melish. **www.collation.folger.edu/2015/08/a-pins-worth-pins-in-books/**

'For a text whose formal complexity anticipated the stream-of-consciousness technique used in *Ulysses* by almost two decades, Arthur Schnitzler's novella *Lieutenant Gustl* seems to have been easygoing for its earliest readers. Soon after it was first published in the Christmas day supplement of the Neue Freie Presse in 1900, army officers in a café on Vienna's Ringstrasse could be seen marking passages in red pencil.'

Leo A. Lensing, 'The officer's new names', **Times Literary Supplement**, 14 October 2011

'To five grammes of mercuric chloride was added sixty drops of creosote, and the mixture was then thinned down in 600cc. of overproof white rum, the cheapest form of alcohol obtainable in the island. This mixture was then brushed on to the spines and the joints of the books. As the treatment has to be repeated every year or so, there was always a team of attendants re-poisoning back-sets of journals. Even though the smell of rum disappeared rapidly, the tang of creosote remained discernible for a long time.'

Roderick Cove,[xi] 'The Scent of Libraries', **The Private Library**,
5th series, Vol.5:3, Autumn 2002, p.143

'The work is based on my collection of second hand "Self help" books. I specifically search out books in which lines or passages of text have been highlighted or underlined by the original owner. The work explores the desire of individuals to reclaim control of different aspects of their life, be it to lose weight, beat depression or to achieve contentment in modern life. The desire to change a trait is the expression of a wish to have more control over day to day existence. For some this desire manifests itself in turning to these books in search of inspirational advice and methodologies to aid achieving these goals. My attention is drawn to the first thing they marked. The work is an exploration of this primary act, the making of a visual aide-memoire, that first inspirational step to regain control.' [xii]

PR for David Blackmore's **'Self Help'**, Schwartz Gallery, London E9, 2010

'The order was enshrined in an Act "for the defacing of images and the bringing in of books of old Service in the Church" in January 1550, which was even more far-reaching. In addition to calling in all "antiphoners, missals, scrayles, processionals, manuals, legends, pyes, portuyses, primers in latin or English, cowchers, journals, or other books…heretofore used for the service of the Church", the Act also ordered the destruction by the end of June of all "images of stone, timber, alabaster or earth, graven carved or painted"'.

Eamon Duffy, **The Stripping of the Altars: Traditional Religion in England, c.1400–c.1580** (New Haven, CT/London: Yale University Press, 1992), p.469

'*Before We Forget* does not present a set of blank pages.
Each journal contains prompts to the owner to make
notes, sketch, paste in, and add recollections of the days,
weeks, and months of the 2020 Covid-19 pandemic.'

www.books-on-books.com/tag/lucy-peltz/

'A work in the exhibition by Angus Fairhurst, *A magazine —
Everything removed except 1cm border*, 2005, comprises, as
it says, a glossy periodical carefully disembowelled with
a scalpel, leaving an empty, floppy framework hanging
gracefully on the gallery wall. It is an unpretentious homage
to Robert Morris's wall-hung felt works of the late 1960s, but
also strangely echoes Michelangelo's self-portrait as flayed
skin in *The Last Judgement*, 1536–41.'

David Briers, 'Undone', **Art Monthly** #342, December–January 2010/11

'The early modern English Bible was formed by centuries of development of the page, and of the compilation and ordering of text into its now familiar form. When the Ferrars cut apart its columns, verses and words to re-order them, they in an important sense continued in the same tradition of *compilatio* and *ordinatio*. When they cut the text block from the margins of New Testaments, separating the text from its surrounding references, it was not to erase the connection but to fulfil it. The mixed text that results—always interrupting itself with alternative versions, including both restatements and disturbing differences—models materially the scriptural imagination of the devout reader. Everything is present at once.'

Paul Dyck, 'A New Kind of Printing: Cutting and Pasting a Book for a King at Little Gidding', **The Library: The Transactions of the Bibliographical Society**, Seventh Series, Vol.9, No.3, September 2008, 306–333 (p.331)

'Beckett wrote *Watt* in successive fixed pages of seven notebooks, pausing to revise and make mathematical calculations and other adjustments. The intra-linear and marginal designs have been compared to the Book of Kells but they serve a different function here. They are neither decoration nor simple distraction; they represent eddies of concentration while composition recovers to advance.'

J. C. C. Mays, **Fredson Bowers and the Irish Wolfhound** (Clonmel: Coracle, 2002), p.7

'Northam has a public library. This burned down in 2005 destroying the building and 90% of the books, in a fire believed to have been caused by the action of a hands-free magnifier on a pile of pamphlets.'

www.en.wikipedia.org/wiki/Northam,_Devon

'Demons, demons, demons.'

Inscribed by Sir Thomas More in his **Common Prayer Book**
while imprisoned in the Tower of London, 1534/35

'One of the most heavily annotated volumes in West's shelves is Ludwig Wittgenstein's *Tractatus Logico-Philosophicus* and its binding was made by the artist himself, who could easily have made the thinker's famous words his own: "The limits of language mean the limit of my world."'

Mark Godfrey & Christine Macel (eds), **Franz West** (London: Tate Publishing, 2018), p.34

'The book of stains is a kind of documentation, though my interest in doing it was not biological or scientific. It is a shallow box of black needle-finished leather.'

Ed Ruscha, 'Ruscha discusses his latest work with Christopher Fox', Alexandra Schwartz (ed.), **Leave Any Information at the Signal: Writings, Interviews, Bits, Pages** (Cambridge, MA/London: MIT Press, 2002), p.32

'On 24 May 2013, a Sina Weibo user named 'Independent Sky Traveller' uploaded an image he said caused him to feel shame and loss of face. A graffito reading 'Ding Jinhao was here' (*Ding Jinhao dao ci yiyou* 丁锦昊到此一游) defaced an ancient frieze at the Luxor Temple complex in Egypt.'

www.thechinastory.org/yearbooks/yearbook-2013/introduction-engineering-chinese-civilisation/ding-jinhao-was-everywhere/

'We learn, for example, that the M6 toll road was built on 2.5 million unsold copies of Mills and Boon romances (which were shredded and mixed with Tarmac and asphalt).'

Peter Straus, 'Bookends', **Times Literary Supplement**,
14 February 2020

'When Katharine Pantzer was preparing the great three-volume *Short-title catalogue of books printed in England, Scotland and Ireland and of English books printed abroad, 1475–1640*, she had such bibliographical problems with the various editions of works of the Rev. Henry Smith (who published many more of his sermons than was strictly necessary) that she expressed her irritation with him by making sure an error appeared in one of the headings for his works. Where he was usually cited as "Smith, Henry, minister", on one page his name appears as "Smith, Henry, monster". It apparently took a certain amount of work on Ms Pantzer's part to make sure this "error" was not corrected during the proof-reading process.'

'On Intentional Errors', **Printing History News**, No.27, Summer 2010

'THE "WICKED" BIBLE, with the infamous omission of the word "not" in the seventh commandment (Exodus xx.14), with part of "The Whole Book of Psalmes" and other leaves bound in, various defects, some loss of text through worming and tears, binding broken, 8vo, Robert Barker, 1631'.

Sotheby's auction catalogue, **English Literature and History**, 1990

'HOROBIN, Pete. DIY Live. Dysart Fife, Scotland: DYSart, n.d. (1983?). 7" sandpaper "record" in paper sleeve, with tipped-on bandage.'

Johan Kugelberg & Jeremy Sanders, **Artists' Book Not Artists' Book** (New York, NY: Boo-Hooray/6 Decades, 2012)

'Several of Newton's books have dog-eared corners, and not just with small, neat, page-marking folds. He would fold over large portions of pages so that the corner pointed to a particular word or passage on the page.'

Christine Megowan. **www.scolarcardiff.wordpress.com** /2018/08/

'Damaged books are disassembled and re-assembled to convey new ways of looking at the book as object. The texture of sawn, cut paper, exposing the nature of the material; reassembling books, "inside out" to focus our understanding of the binding process—and sometimes finding the strange and unexpected. As pages are stacked and reassembled new text emerges at the edge of pages. Manipulation of the edge texts present opportunities to "expose" new messages.'

www.iainmacleod-brudenall.com

'The scrolls have fused together in the heat and can't be unravelled. The litany of unravelling techniques that have been attempted over the years amounts to a comedy of human error. In one case, a papyrus was treated with a mixture of ethanol, glycerine, and warm water. It dried up and then, in slow motion, exploded into more than three hundred pieces.'

Abigail Reynolds, **Lost Libraries: The Ruins of Time** (Berlin: Hatje Cantz Verlag GmbH, 2017), p.216

'*Missae ac Missalis Anatomia* (n.p., 1561). A 172-page Latin missal with a 15-page errata, blamed by its printer on the devil.'

Russell Ash & Brian Lake, **Bizarre Books** (London: Pavilion Books Ltd, 1998), p.197

'Orhan Pamuk's Annotated Copy of The Anatomy of Melancholy (2015). Robert Burton's *The Anatomy of Melancholy*, first published in 1621, went through eight untidy revisions during the author's lifetime. Each edition published in the 17th century responded to popular demand for more copies of the book. However, following the eighth edition in 1676, the book went out of print and fashion for nearly 150 years, not to be revived until 1800 as a historical curiosity. This copy of the fifth edition from 1638 has been rebound and re-margined and bears a number of inconclusive ex-libris stamps. As with most copies of the *Anatomy*, historical and contemporary, the book shows the evidence of wear and tear associated with the anxious browsing of previous readers, insomniacs and nervous self diagnosticians. This copy has been drawn in, painted in, and annotated in by the Turkish Nobel Laureate Orhan Pamuk. The book and drawings by Pamuk are housed in a white clamshell box, custom built for the occasion, with title stamped to spine, Anatomy of Melancholy and full text, "Anatomy of Melancholy/Robert Burton/1638/Orhan Pamuk/2015" stamped to front in brown.'

Courtesy the artist and **Bidoun Projects**

'The books of the Sackler Library have so far been somewhat disappointing when it comes to marginalia, however the wall of the ladies toilet on the ground floor is another matter entirely…'

Lauren Winch, 23 November 2020, **Oxford University Marginalia Facebook** group

'Montaigne's practice of writing in books and using that text to form his own compositions were common in Renaissance culture, as we have seen in the writings of Spenser, John Lilliat, and others. But Montaigne's case is unique in that these activities of "writing in" and "on" books seems to have become implicated in the *Essays*' legacy—the form of exemplarity or prescribed reception embodied in the printed volume.'

Jeffrey Todd Knight, **Bound to Read: Compilation, Collections, and the Making of Renaissance Literature** (Philadelphia, PA: University of Pennsylvania Press, 2013), p.14

'we are particularly interested in the language borne of a certain breed of counterfeit clothing coming out of China that finds errant English in abundant configurations printed across T-shirts'.

Shanzai Lyric

'His typing fell short of the computer age, and his handwriting wandered and blotted its way over the paper as his mind did over a topic: invariably in black ink from a calligraphic pen, it became almost as impenetrable as Pepys's shorthand, and perhaps most akin to cuneiform.'

Obituary of Richard Luckett, Pepys Librarian, Magdalen College, Cambridge (1987–2012); **Daily Telegraph**, 17 December 2020 'all th' *Errata* will appeare at the *end*'.

Francis Quarles, 'On the World', **Divine Fancies Digested
into Epigrammes, Meditations and Observations**
(London: John Marriot, 1641)

'Near Fine in Wraps: shows only the most minute indications of use, BUT SCATTERED HI-LIGHTING THROUGHOUT TEXT and A FEW WORDS IN THE REAR PANEL COVER BLURBS UNDERLINED IN INK; binding square and secure; text clean. Just a hint of wear to extremities; mildest rubbing; pages tanned a bit. Very close to "As New". NOT a Remainder. NOT a Book-Club. NOT Ex-Library copy. 8vo. 291pp.'

Abebooks Purchase Order No.: 65003854

'she pressed her hands to her cheeks to feel how hot they were and then tried to cool them [...] with the cool innards of her A Level Business Studies text book. She was a skinny statuette. She was Tome-Head'. [xiii]

Nicola Barker, **Wide Open** (London: Faber, 1998), p.100

'James R. Page, a former trustee of the Huntington Library,
San Marino, California, and one-time director of Union Oil,
believed the marginalia in his collection of medieval and early
modern texts added to their value.'

Elizabeth Evenden, reviewing William H Sherman's *Used Books:
Marking Readers in Renaissance England* (Philadelphia, PA: University
of Pennsylvania Press, 2007); **English Historical Review**, cxxiv, No.509,
August 2009, 956–958 (p.956)

'In digesting his books and manuscripts Dee employed a number of basic annotational techniques, general categories of marginal notes that are found not only throughout Dee's marginalia but in those of almost all sixteenth-century scholarly readers. The most basic of these is the use of nonverbal marks to draw attention to words or passages—underlinings in the text, or lines, brackets, asterisks, quotation marks, hands with pointing fingers, and so on, in the margin.'

William H. Sherman, **John Dee: The Politics of Reading and Writing in the English Renaissance** (Amherst, MA: University of Massachusetts Press, 1995), p.81

'He cuts out the sections from Giraldus Cambrensis that he quotes in *Coming Down the Wye* to paste into the notebooks he uses; he cuts out illustrations from *The Voyage of HMS Beagle* (1890) to give them to Ralph Beedham to re-ingrave for the Limited Editions Club editions; he cuts out a very ordinary photo of a horse in motion from his large and presumably expensive edition of Muybridge's *Animals in Motion* (1907). There was something that intrigued him in the section on lepers in Parry's photographic collection *Tahiti* (1934), so he slices those pages out with a razor blade.'

Jim Maslen, 'Robert Gibbings: a man and his books', **The Private Library**, 6th series, Vol.1:1, Spring 2008, p.24

'A London businessman who stole and damaged priceless books at the Bodleian Library and British Library has been sentenced to two years in prison. Farhad Hakimzadeh, 60, of Rutland Gardens, pleaded guilty to ten counts of theft at Wood Green Crown Court in August last year, and asked for a further 20 charges to be taken into account including material from the Bodleian Library in Oxford. He mutilated plates and maps from a collection mainly from the 16th, 17th and 18th century, with a lesser number of 19th and 20th century items. Most of the material he tampered with covered the West European engagement with Mesopotamia, Persia and the Mogul empire and western travel, colonisation and exploration.The British Library said Mr Hakimzadeh had "used considerable skill, deceit and determination" in instances which were often difficult to spot."We have zero tolerance of anyone who harms our collections and will pursue anyone who threatens them with utmost vigour," said a spokesperson.'

www.culture24.org.uk/history-and-heritage/literary-history/
art64527

'As a reproduction of a historical artifact, this work may contain missing or blurred pages, poor pictures, errant marks, etc. Scholars believe, and we concur, that this work is important enough to be preserved, reproduced, and made generally available to the public.'

www.amazon.co.uk/Cybele-Britannica-British-Geographical-Relations/dp/134601 325X

'Pen trials, signatures, and ownership marks might jostle against snatches of transcribed sermons, commonplaced passages from other religious books, recipes for ink, or child doodles.'

Michael Durrant, 'Old books, New beginnings: Recovering Lost Pages', **Inscription: The Journal of Material Text—Theory, Practice, History** (York/Leeds: information as material & Leeds Beckett University, 2020), 50–63 (p.50)

'JULY 31, MUNDAY, about 10 of the clock in the morn Andrew Skinner the parator made a fire of two fagots in the Theater yard, and burnt the 2nd volume of Ath. Oxon,—In the Gazet of 3 August is an account of it, but the scandalous places in the book are not pointed at.'

Llewelyn Powys (abridger), **The Life and Times of Anthony à Wood** (Oxford: Department of Design, Oxford Polytechnic, 1975), p.246

'the first quarter of the nineteenth century saw a remarkable efflorescence of quite extraordinary three-dimensional treatments of book spines, in which modest raised bands turned into large excrescences entirely devoid of any reference to function'.

Nicholas Pickwoad, 'The History of the False Raised Band', in Robin Myers, Michael Harris & Giles Mandelbrote (eds), **Against the Law: Crime, Sharp Practice and the Control of Print** (New Castle, DE/ London: Oak Knoll Press & The British Library, 2004), pp.125–27

'At Braziers[xiv] one night he obtained what Jeff Nuttall calls
"an irreplaceable book" belonging to a friend of Trocchi's; a
local source identifies it as *The Brook Kerith* by George Moore,
a novel about the youth of Jesus Christ. Latham plastered
it on to the drawing room wall with Polyfilla. To finish the
work of anti-art he "shot Aerosol over book and wall in a big
explosion", leaving a large black spot.'

James Campbell, 'Culture shock', **Times Literary Supplement**,
8 February 2019

'The monuments of Classical Literature: adored, dead. Traditionally, we bring them back to life by engaging with their time-tested ideas: ideas that have been manufactured and handed down by institutions of learning. A pin-hole view that can also be necrophilic. *It Is Foul Weather In Us All* contests this relationship to received ideas, inviting artists and writers to use Shakespeare—literally. By instructing the participants to leave their copies of *The Tempest* out in the rain, Boglione constructs a transformative reader-writer dialogue that is truly present—what can be more present than our daily weather?'

Robert Fitterman. **www.lightsculpture.pagesperso-orange.fr/ sharon/ma_ bibliotheque.html** 'the book is secured by two large industrial aluminium bolts that when removed allow for the pages to be removed, rearranged, or exhibited individually.'

Fact-sheet for **The Bolted Book** (New York, NY: Designers & Books, 2017), a facsimile reprint of Fortunato Depero's *Depero Futurista* (Milan: Dinamo-Azari, 1927)

'"David, what *have* you been doing tonight?" He moved across the tent and looked over the valise at the packing case-table. The green-bound copy of Sir Thomas Browne, and the notebook into which Barton had earlier copied the quotations, lay in a pile, torn into small pieces, the leaves ripped from the binding. There were only a few pages still left intact, he had almost finished when Hilliard woke.
"You can't make a pattern out of it, you cannot read a book and get comfort from fine words, and great thoughts, and you shouldn't bloody well *try*."'

Susan Hill, **Strange Meeting** (London: Penguin Books Ltd, 1989), p.124

'The Binding of this book is the skin of the Murderer William Corder taken from his body and tanned by myself in the year 1828. George Creed Surgeon to the Suffolk Hospital.'

www.stedmundsbury.gov.uk/sebc/exhibits/ctm

'Police are trying to locate the owner of a 300-year-old ledger, bound in human skin, found in a Leeds road. Written mainly in French, its macabre covering was said to be a regular sight during the French Revolution. In the 18th and 19th Centuries it was common to bind accounts of murder trials in the killer's skin – known as anthropodermic bibliopegy. The book was discovered in The Headrow and may have been discarded after a burglary, detectives said. They said the book may have been stolen in West or North Yorkshire. They are appealing to anyone who may have information, or who may have owned the ledger, to contact them. Many older libraries have examples of anthropodermic bibliopegy in their collection.'

www.news.bbc.co.uk/1/hi/england/west_yorkshire/4891100.stm

'If you mutilate a book, it's not just a cut, the text is mutilated, a vital part is lost, like when you cut an arm or something. Also like the expression of "bleeding" you use in printing—here it's literal, you can see the ink stain from the cut, the text appears to bleed from the mutilation.'

Dora García on her *Ulysses (multiple)*, in conversation with Bryony Bond in **Pages: Future Potentials / Future Legacies** (Leeds: Wild Pansy Press, 2017), p.15

'A velvet-bound copy of a Dictionary of Symbolism
and Historicity translated from the Spanish into English
and devoured by subterranean termites in Greece.
Photo: Rentokil.'

Caption from Ian Breakwell & Paul Hammond (eds), **Brought to
Book: The Balance of Books and Life** (London: Penguin Books Ltd,
1994), p.95

'Sometimes the proof-reading is so spectacularly shoddy
that you wonder whether it's deliberate. In one glorious
paragraph we have repeated occurrences of "Phil Spectre"
and "Don Lett's", and the word used to describe London's
relation to the rest of the country always comes out as
"capitol". Actually, I rather suspect it *is* deliberate: after all,
one of the chief *raisons d'être* of Home's work is to give
offence, and maybe he has hit on this as just another
way to upset his readers.'

Nicholas Lezard, reviewing Stewart Home's novel *Mandy,
Charlie & Mary-Jane* (Los Angeles, CA: Penny-Ante Editions, 2013),
The Guardian, 5 March 2013

'A modified paperback book cover, [xv] picked up in a secondhand book stall under Waterloo Bridge, London. Perhaps doctored by the person behind the signature ('Sato') on the half-title page.'

Andreas Steinbracher, 'You and Me, Gently Touching a Piece of Paper Exercise Instructions for Daily Practice' in John Morgan, **Raum 106, Nr. 1 An Everyday Séance** (Dusseldorf: Kunstakademie, 2018), p.80

'There was an old Man of Vesuvius,
Who studied the works of Vitruvius
But the flames burned his book,
so to drinking he took,
That morbid old man of Vesuvius!'

Edward Lear. **www.gutenberg.org/files/982/
982-h/982-h.htm#2H_4_0052**

'Fillstup.'

James Joyce, **Finnegans Wake**
(London: Faber, 1973), p.20

Endnotes

i   *The Centenary Handbook of the Antiquarian Booksellers Association* (2006), gives this clarification: 'foxing describes the red-brown patches, spotting the smaller dark blemishes' [*sic*].

ii   In conversation with Sheila Markham, the late Niall Devitt spoke candidly about his own approach to making catalogues: 'Cataloguing is a real pleasure, and I like to write something more than the bare details. Most cataloguers don't seem to understand the difference between a list and a catalogue. A list is something you might send to a bookseller, where you have to exercise strict economy over the number of lines. But a catalogue has more of an edge of hard sell to it—you're trying to make something sound attractive by calling attention to points of interest.' www.Sheila-markham.com/interviews/nial-and-margaret-devitt.html

iii   This seller's eBay sales page comes with a quaint disclaimer: 'Please understand that I am not an expert on my books, but am only a lover of old history books and collector. I am always upgrading my collection, so putting my old copies on Ebay. I have done my best to describe this book based on my current knowledge, but nobody is perfect.'

iv   A fiendishly difficult artificial language invented by Johann Martin Schleyer, which was very popular in the 1880s, until largely superceded by Esperanto.

v   Richard Stanyhursts's translation into English hexameters of the first four books of the *Æneid* (1582), was mocked as a grotesque distortion in its day, by the likes of Elizabethan pamphleteer Thomas Nashe, and George Pullenham, that great arbiter of literary decorum.

vi   Tatwine was the tenth Archbishop of Canterbury from AD 731 to 734.

vii   In fact, this is Bolaño's re-enactment of Marcel Duchamp's book work *Unhappy Readymade* (1919/20), the strange nuptial gift to his sister Suzanne, generated by a set of remote instructions cabled from Buenos Aires to Paris.

viii   See my blogpost www.hamp09.wordpress.com/2016/11/28/holocausts-of-the-scrollcodex/

ix   A musician, impresario and humourist, Spiegl arrived in England in 1939 a Jewish refugee from Nazi occupied Austria. Best known as the composer of the theme tune to BBC's *Z-Cars* series, Liverpool became his adopted home, where, from the 1960s, he ran The Scouse Press, a terrace publishing project. In a series of mini books, Spiegl compiled press cuttings sent in by the public, featuring malapropisms, misprints and mondegreens.

x   A digital scan of this fascinating, enlightened report, written by G. Mackenzie Bacon M.D., Medical Superintendent of the Cambridgeshire County Asylum, England, is available at www.publicdomainreview.org/collection/on-the-writing-of-the-insane-1870/

xi   Cove's recollection is of time spent in the library of the Imperial College of Tropical Agriculture, Trinidad.

xii   A sample page in this exhibition, called *Be Your Own Best Friend* (2010), featured an underlined sentence, characterising the art critic as someone who 'will always be on your back like some vicious harpy, undermining your confidence and zest for living'.

xiii   Barker's image quite literally declares that books are cool, and by association evokes Guiseppe Arcimboldo's still life painting *The Librarian* (1621).

xiv   A late seventeenth-century building in the Oxfordshire countryside, remodelled in the Strawberry Hill Gothic style, which became a safe house for Mick Jagger and Keith Richards, after the notorious Redlands drug bust of 1967. Today it is home to the self-styled Braziers Park School of Integrative Research.

xv   The book in question was a very tatty 1969 Pelican edition of R. D. Laing's *The Divided Self*—its cover designed by Martin Bassett— of three overlapping blue, green and yellow circles. The elusive ('Sato'), dreamt up an extension to this Venn arrangement in the form of several smaller, meticulously painted-on black, red and white circles. A low-res monochrome photostat has been stuck to the lower half of the cardboard cover, whose symbolic purpose, if any, is unknown.

Colophon

Against Decorum—Michael Hampton

First published 2022 by
information as material, York, UK

information as material is an independent imprint that publishes work by artists and writers who use extant material —selecting it and reframing it to generate new meanings— and who, in doing so, disrupt the existing order of things.

www.informationasmaterial.org

ISBN: 978-1-907468-39-1

Cataloguing in Publications Data is available on request

Design & typesetting—Groundwork, Skipton

Typeface—Adobe Source Sans 3

Printing & binding—Short Run Press, Exeter

Paper—Pergraphica Classic Smooth 120gsm